My Phone & Address Book

This book belongs to:

Name:_____

Address:_____

Email:_____

Home Phone:_____

Mobile Phone:_____

Work Phone:_____

NAME AND ADDRESS - A	PHONE NUMBER
Name:	Home:
Address:	Mobile:
Email:	Work:
Name:	Home:
Address:	Mobile:
Email:	Work:
Name:	Home:
Address:	Mobile:
Email:	Work:
Name:	Home:
Address:	Mobile:
Email:	Work:
Name:	Home:
Address:	Mobile:
Email:	Work:
Name:	Home:
Address:	Mobile:
Email:	Work:
Name:	Home:
Address:	Mobile:
Email:	Work:
Name:	Home:
Address:	Mobile:
Email:	Work:
Name:	Home:
Address:	Mobile:
Email:	Work:
Name:	Home:
Address:	Mobile:
Email:	Work:

©Lois Eastlund 2018

NAME AND ADDRESS - A   PHONE NUMBER

Name:	Home:
Address:	Mobile:
Email:	Work:
Name:	Home:
Address:	Mobile:
Email:	Work:
Name:	Home:
Address:	Mobile:
Email:	Work:
Name:	Home:
Address:	Mobile:
Email:	Work:
Name:	Home:
Address:	Mobile:
Email:	Work:
Name:	Home:
Address:	Mobile:
Email:	Work:
Name:	Home:
Address:	Mobile:
Email:	Work:
Name:	Home:
Address:	Mobile:
Email:	Work:
Name:	Home:
Address:	Mobile:
Email:	Work:
Name:	Home:
Address:	Mobile:
Email:	Work:

©Lois Eastlund 2018

NAME AND ADDRESS - B   PHONE NUMBER

Name:	Home:
Address:	Mobile:
Email:	Work:
Name:	Home:
Address:	Mobile:
Email:	Work:
Name:	Home:
Address:	Mobile:
Email:	Work:
Name:	Home:
Address:	Mobile:
Email:	Work:
Name:	Home:
Address:	Mobile:
Email:	Work:
Name:	Home:
Address:	Mobile:
Email:	Work:
Name:	Home:
Address:	Mobile:
Email:	Work:
Name:	Home:
Address:	Mobile:
Email:	Work:
Name:	Home:
Address:	Mobile:
Email:	Work:
Name:	Home:
Address:	Mobile:
Email:	Work:

©*Lois Eastlund 2018*

NAME AND ADDRESS - B   PHONE NUMBER

Name:	Home:
Address:	Mobile:
Email:	Work:
Name:	Home:
Address:	Mobile:
Email:	Work:
Name:	Home:
Address:	Mobile:
Email:	Work:
Name:	Home:
Address:	Mobile:
Email:	Work:
Name:	Home:
Address:	Mobile:
Email:	Work:
Name:	Home:
Address:	Mobile:
Email:	Work:
Name:	Home:
Address:	Mobile:
Email:	Work:
Name:	Home:
Address:	Mobile:
Email:	Work:
Name:	Home:
Address:	Mobile:
Email:	Work:

©Lois Eastlund 2018

NAME AND ADDRESS - C   PHONE NUMBER

Name:	Home:
Address:	Mobile:
Email:	Work:
Name:	Home:
Address:	Mobile:
Email:	Work:
Name:	Home:
Address:	Mobile:
Email:	Work:
Name:	Home:
Address:	Mobile:
Email:	Work:
Name:	Home:
Address:	Mobile:
Email:	Work:
Name:	Home:
Address:	Mobile:
Email:	Work:
Name:	Home:
Address:	Mobile:
Email:	Work:
Name:	Home:
Address:	Mobile:
Email:	Work:
Name:	Home:
Address:	Mobile:
Email:	Work:
Name:	Home:
Address:	Mobile:
Email:	Work:

©*Lois Eastlund 2018*

NAME AND ADDRESS - C   PHONE NUMBER

Name:	Home:
Address:	Mobile:
Email:	Work:
Name:	Home:
Address:	Mobile:
Email:	Work:
Name:	Home:
Address:	Mobile:
Email:	Work:
Name:	Home:
Address:	Mobile:
Email:	Work:
Name:	Home:
Address:	Mobile:
Email:	Work:
Name:	Home:
Address:	Mobile:
Email:	Work:
Name:	Home:
Address:	Mobile:
Email:	Work:
Name:	Home:
Address:	Mobile:
Email:	Work:
Name:	Home:
Address:	Mobile:
Email:	Work:
Name:	Home:
Address:	Mobile:
Email:	Work:

©*Lois Eastlund 2018*

NAME AND ADDRESS - D   PHONE NUMBER

Name:	Home:
Address:	Mobile:
Email:	Work:
Name:	Home:
Address:	Mobile:
Email:	Work:
Name:	Home:
Address:	Mobile:
Email:	Work:
Name:	Home:
Address:	Mobile:
Email:	Work:
Name:	Home:
Address:	Mobile:
Email:	Work:
Name:	Home:
Address:	Mobile:
Email:	Work:
Name:	Home:
Address:	Mobile:
Email:	Work:
Name:	Home:
Address:	Mobile:
Email:	Work:
Name:	Home:
Address:	Mobile:
Email:	Work:
Name:	Home:
Address:	Mobile:
Email:	Work:

©Lois Eastlund 2018

NAME AND ADDRESS - D   PHONE NUMBER

Name:	Home:
Address:	Mobile:
Email:	Work:
Name:	Home:
Address:	Mobile:
Email:	Work:
Name:	Home:
Address:	Mobile:
Email:	Work:
Name:	Home:
Address:	Mobile:
Email:	Work:
Name:	Home:
Address:	Mobile:
Email:	Work:
Name:	Home:
Address:	Mobile:
Email:	Work:
Name:	Home:
Address:	Mobile:
Email:	Work:
Name:	Home:
Address:	Mobile:
Email:	Work:
Name:	Home:
Address:	Mobile:
Email:	Work:
Name:	Home:
Address:	Mobile:
Email:	Work:

©Lois Eastlund 2018

NAME AND ADDRESS - E	PHONE NUMBER
Name:	Home:
Address:	Mobile:
Email:	Work:
Name:	Home:
Address:	Mobile:
Email:	Work:
Name:	Home:
Address:	Mobile:
Email:	Work:
Name:	Home:
Address:	Mobile:
Email:	Work:
Name:	Home:
Address:	Mobile:
Email:	Work:
Name:	Home:
Address:	Mobile:
Email:	Work:
Name:	Home:
Address:	Mobile:
Email:	Work:
Name:	Home:
Address:	Mobile:
Email:	Work:
Name:	Home:
Address:	Mobile:
Email:	Work:
Name:	Home:
Address:	Mobile:
Email:	Work:

©Lois Eastlund 2018

NAME AND ADDRESS - E   PHONE NUMBER

Name:	Home:
Address:	Mobile:
Email:	Work:
Name:	Home:
Address:	Mobile:
Email:	Work:
Name:	Home:
Address:	Mobile:
Email:	Work:
Name:	Home:
Address:	Mobile:
Email:	Work:
Name:	Home:
Address:	Mobile:
Email:	Work:
Name:	Home:
Address:	Mobile:
Email:	Work:
Name:	Home:
Address:	Mobile:
Email:	Work:
Name:	Home:
Address:	Mobile:
Email:	Work:
Name:	Home:
Address:	Mobile:
Email:	Work:
Name:	Home:
Address:	Mobile:
Email:	Work:

©Lois Eastlund 2018

NAME AND ADDRESS - F   PHONE NUMBER

Name:	Home:
Address:	Mobile:
Email:	Work:
Name:	Home:
Address:	Mobile:
Email:	Work:
Name:	Home:
Address:	Mobile:
Email:	Work:
Name:	Home:
Address:	Mobile:
Email:	Work:
Name:	Home:
Address:	Mobile:
Email:	Work:
Name:	Home:
Address:	Mobile:
Email:	Work:
Name:	Home:
Address:	Mobile:
Email:	Work:
Name:	Home:
Address:	Mobile:
Email:	Work:
Name:	Home:
Address:	Mobile:
Email:	Work:
Name:	Home:
Address:	Mobile:
Email:	Work:

©Lois Eastlund 2018

NAME AND ADDRESS - F   PHONE NUMBER

Name:	Home:
Address:	Mobile:
Email:	Work:
Name:	Home:
Address:	Mobile:
Email:	Work:
Name:	Home:
Address:	Mobile:
Email:	Work:
Name:	Home:
Address:	Mobile:
Email:	Work:
Name:	Home:
Address:	Mobile:
Email:	Work:
Name:	Home:
Address:	Mobile:
Email:	Work:
Name:	Home:
Address:	Mobile:
Email:	Work:
Name:	Home:
Address:	Mobile:
Email:	Work:
Name:	Home:
Address:	Mobile:
Email:	Work:
Name:	Home:
Address:	Mobile:
Email:	Work:

©*Lois Eastlund 2018*

NAME AND ADDRESS - G   PHONE NUMBER

Name:	Home:
Address:	Mobile:
Email:	Work:
Name:	Home:
Address:	Mobile:
Email:	Work:
Name:	Home:
Address:	Mobile:
Email:	Work:
Name:	Home:
Address:	Mobile:
Email:	Work:
Name:	Home:
Address:	Mobile:
Email:	Work:
Name:	Home:
Address:	Mobile:
Email:	Work:
Name:	Home:
Address:	Mobile:
Email:	Work:
Name:	Home:
Address:	Mobile:
Email:	Work:
Name:	Home:
Address:	Mobile:
Email:	Work:
Name:	Home:
Address:	Mobile:
Email:	Work:

©*Lois Eastlund 2018*

NAME AND ADDRESS - G   PHONE NUMBER

Name:	Home:
Address:	Mobile:
Email:	Work:
Name:	Home:
Address:	Mobile:
Email:	Work:
Name:	Home:
Address:	Mobile:
Email:	Work:
Name:	Home:
Address:	Mobile:
Email:	Work:
Name:	Home:
Address:	Mobile:
Email:	Work:
Name:	Home:
Address:	Mobile:
Email:	Work:
Name:	Home:
Address:	Mobile:
Email:	Work:
Name:	Home:
Address:	Mobile:
Email:	Work:
Name:	Home:
Address:	Mobile:
Email:	Work:

©Lois Eastlund 2018

NAME AND ADDRESS - H	PHONE NUMBER
Name:	Home:
Address:	Mobile:
Email:	Work:
Name:	Home:
Address:	Mobile:
Email:	Work:
Name:	Home:
Address:	Mobile:
Email:	Work:
Name:	Home:
Address:	Mobile:
Email:	Work:
Name:	Home:
Address:	Mobile:
Email:	Work:
Name:	Home:
Address:	Mobile:
Email:	Work:
Name:	Home:
Address:	Mobile:
Email:	Work:
Name:	Home:
Address:	Mobile:
Email:	Work:
Name:	Home:
Address:	Mobile:
Email:	Work:
Name:	Home:
Address:	Mobile:
Email:	Work:

©Lois Eastlund 2018

NAME AND ADDRESS - H   PHONE NUMBER

Name:	Home:
Address:	Mobile:
Email:	Work:
Name:	Home:
Address:	Mobile:
Email:	Work:
Name:	Home:
Address:	Mobile:
Email:	Work:
Name:	Home:
Address:	Mobile:
Email:	Work:
Name:	Home:
Address:	Mobile:
Email:	Work:
Name:	Home:
Address:	Mobile:
Email:	Work:
Name:	Home:
Address:	Mobile:
Email:	Work:
Name:	Home:
Address:	Mobile:
Email:	Work:
Name:	Home:
Address:	Mobile:
Email:	Work:
Name:	Home:
Address:	Mobile:
Email:	Work:

©Lois Eastlund 2018

NAME AND ADDRESS - I	PHONE NUMBER
Name:	Home:
Address:	Mobile:
Email:	Work:
Name:	Home:
Address:	Mobile:
Email:	Work:
Name:	Home:
Address:	Mobile:
Email:	Work:
Name:	Home:
Address:	Mobile:
Email:	Work:
Name:	Home:
Address:	Mobile:
Email:	Work:
Name:	Home:
Address:	Mobile:
Email:	Work:
Name:	Home:
Address:	Mobile:
Email:	Work:
Name:	Home:
Address:	Mobile:
Email:	Work:
Name:	Home:
Address:	Mobile:
Email:	Work:
Name:	Home:
Address:	Mobile:
Email:	Work:

©Lois Eastlund 2018

NAME AND ADDRESS - I   PHONE NUMBER

Name:	Home:
Address:	Mobile:
Email:	Work:
Name:	Home:
Address:	Mobile:
Email:	Work:
Name:	Home:
Address:	Mobile:
Email:	Work:
Name:	Home:
Address:	Mobile:
Email:	Work:
Name:	Home:
Address:	Mobile:
Email:	Work:
Name:	Home:
Address:	Mobile:
Email:	Work:
Name:	Home:
Address:	Mobile:
Email:	Work:
Name:	Home:
Address:	Mobile:
Email:	Work:
Name:	Home:
Address:	Mobile:
Email:	Work:
Name:	Home:
Address:	Mobile:
Email:	Work:

©*Lois Eastlund 2018*

NAME AND ADDRESS - J   PHONE NUMBER

Name:	Home:
Address:	Mobile:
Email:	Work:
Name:	Home:
Address:	Mobile:
Email:	Work:
Name:	Home:
Address:	Mobile:
Email:	Work:
Name:	Home:
Address:	Mobile:
Email:	Work:
Name:	Home:
Address:	Mobile:
Email:	Work:
Name:	Home:
Address:	Mobile:
Email:	Work:
Name:	Home:
Address:	Mobile:
Email:	Work:
Name:	Home:
Address:	Mobile:
Email:	Work:
Name:	Home:
Address:	Mobile:
Email:	Work:
Name:	Home:
Address:	Mobile:
Email:	Work:

©Lois Eastlund 2018

NAME AND ADDRESS - J   PHONE NUMBER

Name:	Home:
Address:	Mobile:
Email:	Work:
Name:	Home:
Address:	Mobile:
Email:	Work:
Name:	Home:
Address:	Mobile:
Email:	Work:
Name:	Home:
Address:	Mobile:
Email:	Work:
Name:	Home:
Address:	Mobile:
Email:	Work:
Name:	Home:
Address:	Mobile:
Email:	Work:
Name:	Home:
Address:	Mobile:
Email:	Work:
Name:	Home:
Address:	Mobile:
Email:	Work:
Name:	Home:
Address:	Mobile:
Email:	Work:
Name:	Home:
Address:	Mobile:
Email:	Work:

©Lois Eastlund 2018

NAME AND ADDRESS · K   PHONE NUMBER

Name:	Home:
Address:	Mobile:
Email:	Work:
Name:	Home:
Address:	Mobile:
Email:	Work:
Name:	Home:
Address:	Mobile:
Email:	Work:
Name:	Home:
Address:	Mobile:
Email:	Work:
Name:	Home:
Address:	Mobile:
Email:	Work:
Name:	Home:
Address:	Mobile:
Email:	Work:
Name:	Home:
Address:	Mobile:
Email:	Work:
Name:	Home:
Address:	Mobile:
Email:	Work:
Name:	Home:
Address:	Mobile:
Email:	Work:
Name:	Home:
Address:	Mobile:
Email:	Work:

©Lois Eastlund 2018

NAME AND ADDRESS - K   PHONE NUMBER

Name:	Home:
Address:	Mobile:
Email:	Work:
Name:	Home:
Address:	Mobile:
Email:	Work:
Name:	Home:
Address:	Mobile:
Email:	Work:
Name:	Home:
Address:	Mobile:
Email:	Work:
Name:	Home:
Address:	Mobile:
Email:	Work:
Name:	Home:
Address:	Mobile:
Email:	Work:
Name:	Home:
Address:	Mobile:
Email:	Work:
Name:	Home:
Address:	Mobile:
Email:	Work:
Name:	Home:
Address:	Mobile:
Email:	Work:
Name:	Home:
Address:	Mobile:
Email:	Work:

©Lois Eastlund 2018

NAME AND ADDRESS - L	PHONE NUMBER
Name:	Home:
Address:	Mobile:
Email:	Work:
Name:	Home:
Address:	Mobile:
Email:	Work:
Name:	Home:
Address:	Mobile:
Email:	Work:
Name:	Home:
Address:	Mobile:
Email:	Work:
Name:	Home:
Address:	Mobile:
Email:	Work:
Name:	Home:
Address:	Mobile:
Email:	Work:
Name:	Home:
Address:	Mobile:
Email:	Work:
Name:	Home:
Address:	Mobile:
Email:	Work:
Name:	Home:
Address:	Mobile:
Email:	Work:
Name:	Home:
Address:	Mobile:
Email:	Work:

©*Lois Eastlund 2018*

NAME AND ADDRESS - L	PHONE NUMBER
Name:	Home:
Address:	Mobile:
Email:	Work:
Name:	Home:
Address:	Mobile:
Email:	Work:
Name:	Home:
Address:	Mobile:
Email:	Work:
Name:	Home:
Address:	Mobile:
Email:	Work:
Name:	Home:
Address:	Mobile:
Email:	Work:
Name:	Home:
Address:	Mobile:
Email:	Work:
Name:	Home:
Address:	Mobile:
Email:	Work:
Name:	Home:
Address:	Mobile:
Email:	Work:
Name:	Home:
Address:	Mobile:
Email:	Work:
Name:	Home:
Address:	Mobile:
Email:	Work:

©Lois Eastlund 2018

NAME AND ADDRESS - M   PHONE NUMBER

Name:	Home:
Address:	Mobile:
Email:	Work:
Name:	Home:
Address:	Mobile:
Email:	Work:
Name:	Home:
Address:	Mobile:
Email:	Work:
Name:	Home:
Address:	Mobile:
Email:	Work:
Name:	Home:
Address:	Mobile:
Email:	Work:
Name:	Home:
Address:	Mobile:
Email:	Work:
Name:	Home:
Address:	Mobile:
Email:	Work:
Name:	Home:
Address:	Mobile:
Email:	Work:
Name:	Home:
Address:	Mobile:
Email:	Work:
Name:	Home:
Address:	Mobile:
Email:	Work:

©Lois Eastlund 2018

NAME AND ADDRESS - M   PHONE NUMBER

Name:	Home:
Address:	Mobile:
Email:	Work:
Name:	Home:
Address:	Mobile:
Email:	Work:
Name:	Home:
Address:	Mobile:
Email:	Work:
Name:	Home:
Address:	Mobile:
Email:	Work:
Name:	Home:
Address:	Mobile:
Email:	Work:
Name:	Home:
Address:	Mobile:
Email:	Work:
Name:	Home:
Address:	Mobile:
Email:	Work:
Name:	Home:
Address:	Mobile:
Email:	Work:
Name:	Home:
Address:	Mobile:
Email:	Work:
Name:	Home:
Address:	Mobile:
Email:	Work:

©Lois Eastlund 2018

NAME AND ADDRESS - N   PHONE NUMBER

Name:	Home:
Address:	Mobile:
Email:	Work:
Name:	Home:
Address:	Mobile:
Email:	Work:
Name:	Home:
Address:	Mobile:
Email:	Work:
Name:	Home:
Address:	Mobile:
Email:	Work:
Name:	Home:
Address:	Mobile:
Email:	Work:
Name:	Home:
Address:	Mobile:
Email:	Work:
Name:	Home:
Address:	Mobile:
Email:	Work:
Name:	Home:
Address:	Mobile:
Email:	Work:
Name:	Home:
Address:	Mobile:
Email:	Work:
Name:	Home:
Address:	Mobile:
Email:	Work:

©*Lois Eastlund 2018*

NAME AND ADDRESS - N	PHONE NUMBER
Name:	Home:
Address:	Mobile:
Email:	Work:
Name:	Home:
Address:	Mobile:
Email:	Work:
Name:	Home:
Address:	Mobile:
Email:	Work:
Name:	Home:
Address:	Mobile:
Email:	Work:
Name:	Home:
Address:	Mobile:
Email:	Work:
Name:	Home:
Address:	Mobile:
Email:	Work:
Name:	Home:
Address:	Mobile:
Email:	Work:
Name:	Home:
Address:	Mobile:
Email:	Work:
Name:	Home:
Address:	Mobile:
Email:	Work:
Name:	Home:
Address:	Mobile:
Email:	Work:

©*Lois Eastlund 2018*

NAME AND ADDRESS - O	PHONE NUMBER
Name:	Home:
Address:	Mobile:
Email:	Work:
Name:	Home:
Address:	Mobile:
Email:	Work:
Name:	Home:
Address:	Mobile:
Email:	Work:
Name:	Home:
Address:	Mobile:
Email:	Work:
Name:	Home:
Address:	Mobile:
Email:	Work:
Name:	Home:
Address:	Mobile:
Email:	Work:
Name:	Home:
Address:	Mobile:
Email:	Work:
Name:	Home:
Address:	Mobile:
Email:	Work:
Name:	Home:
Address:	Mobile:
Email:	Work:
Name:	Home:
Address:	Mobile:
Email:	Work:

©Lois Eastlund 2018

NAME AND ADDRESS · O

PHONE NUMBER

Name:	Home:
Address:	Mobile:
Email:	Work:
Name:	Home:
Address:	Mobile:
Email:	Work:
Name:	Home:
Address:	Mobile:
Email:	Work:
Name:	Home:
Address:	Mobile:
Email:	Work:
Name:	Home:
Address:	Mobile:
Email:	Work:
Name:	Home:
Address:	Mobile:
Email:	Work:
Name:	Home:
Address:	Mobile:
Email:	Work:
Name:	Home:
Address:	Mobile:
Email:	Work:
Name:	Home:
Address:	Mobile:
Email:	Work:
Name:	Home:
Address:	Mobile:
Email:	Work:

©Lois Eastlund 2018

NAME AND ADDRESS - P

PHONE NUMBER

Name:	Home:
Address:	Mobile:
Email:	Work:
Name:	Home:
Address:	Mobile:
Email:	Work:
Name:	Home:
Address:	Mobile:
Email:	Work:
Name:	Home:
Address:	Mobile:
Email:	Work:
Name:	Home:
Address:	Mobile:
Email:	Work:
Name:	Home:
Address:	Mobile:
Email:	Work:
Name:	Home:
Address:	Mobile:
Email:	Work:
Name:	Home:
Address:	Mobile:
Email:	Work:
Name:	Home:
Address:	Mobile:
Email:	Work:
Name:	Home:
Address:	Mobile:
Email:	Work:

©Lois Eastlund 2018

NAME AND ADDRESS - P   PHONE NUMBER

Name:	Home:
Address:	Mobile:
Email:	Work:
Name:	Home:
Address:	Mobile:
Email:	Work:
Name:	Home:
Address:	Mobile:
Email:	Work:
Name:	Home:
Address:	Mobile:
Email:	Work:
Name:	Home:
Address:	Mobile:
Email:	Work:
Name:	Home:
Address:	Mobile:
Email:	Work:
Name:	Home:
Address:	Mobile:
Email:	Work:
Name:	Home:
Address:	Mobile:
Email:	Work:
Name:	Home:
Address:	Mobile:
Email:	Work:
Name:	Home:
Address:	Mobile:
Email:	Work:

©*Lois Eastlund 2018*

NAME AND ADDRESS - Q	PHONE NUMBER
Name:	Home:
Address:	Mobile:
Email:	Work:
Name:	Home:
Address:	Mobile:
Email:	Work:
Name:	Home:
Address:	Mobile:
Email:	Work:
Name:	Home:
Address:	Mobile:
Email:	Work:
Name:	Home:
Address:	Mobile:
Email:	Work:
Name:	Home:
Address:	Mobile:
Email:	Work:
Name:	Home:
Address:	Mobile:
Email:	Work:
Name:	Home:
Address:	Mobile:
Email:	Work:
Name:	Home:
Address:	Mobile:
Email:	Work:
Name:	Home:
Address:	Mobile:
Email:	Work:

©*Lois Eastlund 2018*

NAME AND ADDRESS - Q   PHONE NUMBER

Name:	Home:
Address:	Mobile:
Email:	Work:
Name:	Home:
Address:	Mobile:
Email:	Work:
Name:	Home:
Address:	Mobile:
Email:	Work:
Name:	Home:
Address:	Mobile:
Email:	Work:
Name:	Home:
Address:	Mobile:
Email:	Work:
Name:	Home:
Address:	Mobile:
Email:	Work:
Name:	Home:
Address:	Mobile:
Email:	Work:
Name:	Home:
Address:	Mobile:
Email:	Work:
Name:	Home:
Address:	Mobile:
Email:	Work:
Name:	Home:
Address:	Mobile:
Email:	Work:

©Lois Eastlund 2018

NAME AND ADDRESS - R

PHONE NUMBER

Name:	Home:
Address:	Mobile:
Email:	Work:
Name:	Home:
Address:	Mobile:
Email:	Work:
Name:	Home:
Address:	Mobile:
Email:	Work:
Name:	Home:
Address:	Mobile:
Email:	Work:
Name:	Home:
Address:	Mobile:
Email:	Work:
Name:	Home:
Address:	Mobile:
Email:	Work:
Name:	Home:
Address:	Mobile:
Email:	Work:
Name:	Home:
Address:	Mobile:
Email:	Work:
Name:	Home:
Address:	Mobile:
Email:	Work:
Name:	Home:
Address:	Mobile:
Email:	Work:

©Lois Eastlund 2018

NAME AND ADDRESS · R   PHONE NUMBER

Name:	Home:
Address:	Mobile:
Email:	Work:
Name:	Home:
Address:	Mobile:
Email:	Work:
Name:	Home:
Address:	Mobile:
Email:	Work:
Name:	Home:
Address:	Mobile:
Email:	Work:
Name:	Home:
Address:	Mobile:
Email:	Work:
Name:	Home:
Address:	Mobile:
Email:	Work:
Name:	Home:
Address:	Mobile:
Email:	Work:
Name:	Home:
Address:	Mobile:
Email:	Work:
Name:	Home:
Address:	Mobile:
Email:	Work:
Name:	Home:
Address:	Mobile:
Email:	Work:

©Lois Eastlund 2018

NAME AND ADDRESS - S	PHONE NUMBER
Name:	Home:
Address:	Mobile:
Email:	Work:
Name:	Home:
Address:	Mobile:
Email:	Work:
Name:	Home:
Address:	Mobile:
Email:	Work:
Name:	Home:
Address:	Mobile:
Email:	Work:
Name:	Home:
Address:	Mobile:
Email:	Work:
Name:	Home:
Address:	Mobile:
Email:	Work:
Name:	Home:
Address:	Mobile:
Email:	Work:
Name:	Home:
Address:	Mobile:
Email:	Work:
Name:	Home:
Address:	Mobile:
Email:	Work:
Name:	Home:
Address:	Mobile:
Email:	Work:

©*Lois Eastlund 2018*

NAME AND ADDRESS - S	**PHONE NUMBER**
Name:	Home:
Address:	Mobile:
Email:	Work:
Name:	Home:
Address:	Mobile:
Email:	Work:
Name:	Home:
Address:	Mobile:
Email:	Work:
Name:	Home:
Address:	Mobile:
Email:	Work:
Name:	Home:
Address:	Mobile:
Email:	Work:
Name:	Home:
Address:	Mobile:
Email:	Work:
Name:	Home:
Address:	Mobile:
Email:	Work:
Name:	Home:
Address:	Mobile:
Email:	Work:
Name:	Home:
Address:	Mobile:
Email:	Work:
Name:	Home:
Address:	Mobile:
Email:	Work:

©*Lois Eastlund 2018*

NAME AND ADDRESS - T   PHONE NUMBER

Name:	Home:
Address:	Mobile:
Email:	Work:
Name:	Home:
Address:	Mobile:
Email:	Work:
Name:	Home:
Address:	Mobile:
Email:	Work:
Name:	Home:
Address:	Mobile:
Email:	Work:
Name:	Home:
Address:	Mobile:
Email:	Work:
Name:	Home:
Address:	Mobile:
Email:	Work:
Name:	Home:
Address:	Mobile:
Email:	Work:
Name:	Home:
Address:	Mobile:
Email:	Work:
Name:	Home:
Address:	Mobile:
Email:	Work:
Name:	Home:
Address:	Mobile:
Email:	Work:

©Lois Eastlund 2018

NAME AND ADDRESS - T   PHONE NUMBER

Name:	Home:
Address:	Mobile:
Email:	Work:
Name:	Home:
Address:	Mobile:
Email:	Work:
Name:	Home:
Address:	Mobile:
Email:	Work:
Name:	Home:
Address:	Mobile:
Email:	Work:
Name:	Home:
Address:	Mobile:
Email:	Work:
Name:	Home:
Address:	Mobile:
Email:	Work:
Name:	Home:
Address:	Mobile:
Email:	Work:
Name:	Home:
Address:	Mobile:
Email:	Work:
Name:	Home:
Address:	Mobile:
Email:	Work:
Name:	Home:
Address:	Mobile:
Email:	Work:

©*Lois Eastlund 2018*

NAME AND ADDRESS - U	PHONE NUMBER
Name:	Home:
Address:	Mobile:
Email:	Work:
Name:	Home:
Address:	Mobile:
Email:	Work:
Name:	Home:
Address:	Mobile:
Email:	Work:
Name:	Home:
Address:	Mobile:
Email:	Work:
Name:	Home:
Address:	Mobile:
Email:	Work:
Name:	Home:
Address:	Mobile:
Email:	Work:
Name:	Home:
Address:	Mobile:
Email:	Work:
Name:	Home:
Address:	Mobile:
Email:	Work:
Name:	Home:
Address:	Mobile:
Email:	Work:
Name:	Home:
Address:	Mobile:
Email:	Work:

©Lois Eastlund 2018

NAME AND ADDRESS · U   PHONE NUMBER

Name:	Home:
Address:	Mobile:
Email:	Work:
Name:	Home:
Address:	Mobile:
Email:	Work:
Name:	Home:
Address:	Mobile:
Email:	Work:
Name:	Home:
Address:	Mobile:
Email:	Work:
Name:	Home:
Address:	Mobile:
Email:	Work:
Name:	Home:
Address:	Mobile:
Email:	Work:
Name:	Home:
Address:	Mobile:
Email:	Work:
Name:	Home:
Address:	Mobile:
Email:	Work:
Name:	Home:
Address:	Mobile:
Email:	Work:

©Lois Eastlund 2018

NAME AND ADDRESS - V	PHONE NUMBER
Name:	Home:
Address:	Mobile:
Email:	Work:
Name:	Home:
Address:	Mobile:
Email:	Work:
Name:	Home:
Address:	Mobile:
Email:	Work:
Name:	Home:
Address:	Mobile:
Email:	Work:
Name:	Home:
Address:	Mobile:
Email:	Work:
Name:	Home:
Address:	Mobile:
Email:	Work:
Name:	Home:
Address:	Mobile:
Email:	Work:
Name:	Home:
Address:	Mobile:
Email:	Work:
Name:	Home:
Address:	Mobile:
Email:	Work:
Name:	Home:
Address:	Mobile:
Email:	Work:

©*Lois Eastlund 2018*

NAME AND ADDRESS - V   PHONE NUMBER

Name:	Home:
Address:	Mobile:
Email:	Work:
Name:	Home:
Address:	Mobile:
Email:	Work:
Name:	Home:
Address:	Mobile:
Email:	Work:
Name:	Home:
Address:	Mobile:
Email:	Work:
Name:	Home:
Address:	Mobile:
Email:	Work:
Name:	Home:
Address:	Mobile:
Email:	Work:
Name:	Home:
Address:	Mobile:
Email:	Work:
Name:	Home:
Address:	Mobile:
Email:	Work:
Name:	Home:
Address:	Mobile:
Email:	Work:
Name:	Home:
Address:	Mobile:
Email:	Work:

©*Lois Eastlund 2018*

NAME AND ADDRESS · W   PHONE NUMBER

Name:	Home:
Address:	Mobile:
Email:	Work:
Name:	Home:
Address:	Mobile:
Email:	Work:
Name:	Home:
Address:	Mobile:
Email:	Work:
Name:	Home:
Address:	Mobile:
Email:	Work:
Name:	Home:
Address:	Mobile:
Email:	Work:
Name:	Home:
Address:	Mobile:
Email:	Work:
Name:	Home:
Address:	Mobile:
Email:	Work:
Name:	Home:
Address:	Mobile:
Email:	Work:
Name:	Home:
Address:	Mobile:
Email:	Work:
Name:	Home:
Address:	Mobile:
Email:	Work:

©*Lois Eastlund 2018*

NAME AND ADDRESS - W   PHONE NUMBER

Name:	Home:
Address:	Mobile:
Email:	Work:
Name:	Home:
Address:	Mobile:
Email:	Work:
Name:	Home:
Address:	Mobile:
Email:	Work:
Name:	Home:
Address:	Mobile:
Email:	Work:
Name:	Home:
Address:	Mobile:
Email:	Work:
Name:	Home:
Address:	Mobile:
Email:	Work:
Name:	Home:
Address:	Mobile:
Email:	Work:
Name:	Home:
Address:	Mobile:
Email:	Work:
Name:	Home:
Address:	Mobile:
Email:	Work:
Name:	Home:
Address:	Mobile:
Email:	Work:

©*Lois Eastlund 2018*

NAME AND ADDRESS - X	PHONE NUMBER
Name:	Home:
Address:	Mobile:
Email:	Work:
Name:	Home:
Address:	Mobile:
Email:	Work:
Name:	Home:
Address:	Mobile:
Email:	Work:
Name:	Home:
Address:	Mobile:
Email:	Work:
Name:	Home:
Address:	Mobile:
Email:	Work:
Name:	Home:
Address:	Mobile:
Email:	Work:
Name:	Home:
Address:	Mobile:
Email:	Work:
Name:	Home:
Address:	Mobile:
Email:	Work:
Name:	Home:
Address:	Mobile:
Email:	Work:
Name:	Home:
Address:	Mobile:
Email:	Work:

©*Lois Eastlund 2018*

NAME AND ADDRESS · X

PHONE NUMBER

Name:	Home:
Address:	Mobile:
Email:	Work:
Name:	Home:
Address:	Mobile:
Email:	Work:
Name:	Home:
Address:	Mobile:
Email:	Work:
Name:	Home:
Address:	Mobile:
Email:	Work:
Name:	Home:
Address:	Mobile:
Email:	Work:
Name:	Home:
Address:	Mobile:
Email:	Work:
Name:	Home:
Address:	Mobile:
Email:	Work:
Name:	Home:
Address:	Mobile:
Email:	Work:
Name:	Home:
Address:	Mobile:
Email:	Work:
Name:	Home:
Address:	Mobile:
Email:	Work:

©Lois Eastlund 2018

NAME AND ADDRESS - Y	PHONE NUMBER
Name:	Home:
Address:	Mobile:
Email:	Work:
Name:	Home:
Address:	Mobile:
Email:	Work:
Name:	Home:
Address:	Mobile:
Email:	Work:
Name:	Home:
Address:	Mobile:
Email:	Work:
Name:	Home:
Address:	Mobile:
Email:	Work:
Name:	Home:
Address:	Mobile:
Email:	Work:
Name:	Home:
Address:	Mobile:
Email:	Work:
Name:	Home:
Address:	Mobile:
Email:	Work:
Name:	Home:
Address:	Mobile:
Email:	Work:
Name:	Home:
Address:	Mobile:
Email:	Work:

©*Lois Eastlund 2018*

NAME AND ADDRESS - Y   PHONE NUMBER

Name:	Home:
Address:	Mobile:
Email:	Work:
Name:	Home:
Address:	Mobile:
Email:	Work:
Name:	Home:
Address:	Mobile:
Email:	Work:
Name:	Home:
Address:	Mobile:
Email:	Work:
Name:	Home:
Address:	Mobile:
Email:	Work:
Name:	Home:
Address:	Mobile:
Email:	Work:
Name:	Home:
Address:	Mobile:
Email:	Work:
Name:	Home:
Address:	Mobile:
Email:	Work:
Name:	Home:
Address:	Mobile:
Email:	Work:

©*Lois Eastlund 2018*

NAME AND ADDRESS - Z   PHONE NUMBER

Name:	Home:
Address:	Mobile:
Email:	Work:
Name:	Home:
Address:	Mobile:
Email:	Work:
Name:	Home:
Address:	Mobile:
Email:	Work:
Name:	Home:
Address:	Mobile:
Email:	Work:
Name:	Home:
Address:	Mobile:
Email:	Work:
Name:	Home:
Address:	Mobile:
Email:	Work:
Name:	Home:
Address:	Mobile:
Email:	Work:
Name:	Home:
Address:	Mobile:
Email:	Work:
Name:	Home:
Address:	Mobile:
Email:	Work:
Name:	Home:
Address:	Mobile:
Email:	Work:

©Lois Eastlund 2018

NAME AND ADDRESS - Z   PHONE NUMBER

Name:	Home:
Address:	Mobile:
Email:	Work:
Name:	Home:
Address:	Mobile:
Email:	Work:
Name:	Home:
Address:	Mobile:
Email:	Work:
Name:	Home:
Address:	Mobile:
Email:	Work:
Name:	Home:
Address:	Mobile:
Email:	Work:
Name:	Home:
Address:	Mobile:
Email:	Work:
Name:	Home:
Address:	Mobile:
Email:	Work:
Name:	Home:
Address:	Mobile:
Email:	Work:
Name:	Home:
Address:	Mobile:
Email:	Work:
Name:	Home:
Address:	Mobile:
Email:	Work:

©*Lois Eastlund 2018*

©*Lois Eastlund 2018*